HOW TO INVEST IN THE

JAMAICAN STOCK MARKET:

FOR BEGINNERS

BY OROY B. CAMPBELL

ACKNOWLEDGEMENT

Firstly, I would like to thank the most-high God for affording me the privilege to share my experiences with you. The journey of the stock market has been up and down, but very satisfying overall. Writing this book has been a journey in and of itself. One that has presented many hurdles in my way, of which I have managed to clear in order to bring this book to you. But I never did this on my own; I got help of which I am very grateful.

Secondly, I would like to take time out to thank my friends and colleagues who supported me on this journey. Whether it be through encouragement or even through peer reviewing. In saying that, there are a few notable mentions for this work. I would like to thank Romario Lee for being a good support and peer reviewer, Latavis and Travis Gray for being peer reviewers also and Chris-Anthony Pinnock for doing such a great cover design.

Thirdly, I am thanking you, yes you. For making that step of believing in what I have to offer by purchasing this book. The road of a serious investor is paved with mistakes and temptations, but I hope this book can steady your path.

"What is your WHY"

By Fabian A. Gordon

Before I go any further, I would like to introduce you to a book that is geared towards personal development. I am a person that loves to develop and if you like the same, then you should love this book.

I have come to the realisation that by complaining too much, you will repel the persons who can help you. Because there are many things that this life will offer as reasonable means that can be justified as good excuses or reasons to murmur; especially when you have all right to. However, here's the thing. The truth is, you either become weaker or stronger in the places that were broken and that's the choice of how WE react or respond moving forward.

In this book, Gordon asked a series of questions while sharing his life story.

1. *Why do you want to give up?*

2. *Why do you even doubt yourself?*

3. *Why are you not giving your goals, dreams and ideas that were given to you by God Almighty 100%!?*

He then went on to ask:

- *Why do YOU want to be successful?*

- *Why are you doing whatever it is that you're doing, and why do you want it so bad?*

- *Why should it be you and not anybody else?*

As a matter of fact, why do you keep on pushing, why do you keep on going? Why don't you just walk away and throw in your towel in this ring called life?

If you can find that reason, that WHY. Life will welcome you to the other side where only a few reside. Because if you know WHY for living, you can endure anyhow.

INTRODUCTION

If you are reading this then you have made the conscious decision to improve your financial situation; an act that I fully support. I started out just like you, eager to invest but with little to no guidance at first and no concrete guide to the Jamaican stock market. So, if you haven't figured it out yet, I have taken it upon myself to provide such a book that takes you from wanting to be an investor to being one, and a successful one at that too!!! Before you go any further, it is imperative for me that you understand that my knowledge and recommendations are not coming from me going to school and getting an investing certificate. Even though I have a degree in Bachelor of Science (Operations Management); this is from trial and error, and experience garnered from basically throwing myself in the line of fire. Which, in my opinion, is one of the best ways to learn. I am not the first to write a book without any traditional schooling on the topic. American businessman Robert E. Kiyosaki, the author of the well-known best seller, 'Rich Dad Poor Dad', one of the wealthiest men in the world; had the same beginning as I. I have read and listened to many financial literacy books to guide me along my path of increasing wealth and looking towards a brighter future. Some of these books include: 'Think and Grow Rich', 'The Richest Man in Babylon', 'Rich Dad Poor Dad' and 'The Cash Flow Quadrant'. They are of written by Americans in an American economy and structure but possess great insights that I assure you, if followed, will make you better equipped for money management and to become financially literate.

You may be wondering when I am going to get to the good stuff; don't worry I am about to right now.

THE JAMAICA STOCK EXCHANGE (JSE)

First, what is an exchange? Put simply, an exchange is an institution, organization, or association which hosts a market where stocks, bonds, options, futures, and financial commodities are traded. Buyers and sellers come together to trade during specific hours on business days. Exchanges impose rules and regulations on the firms and brokers that are involved with them. If a company is traded on an exchange, it is referred to as "listed."

WHAT IS THE PURPOSE OF A STOCK EXCHANGE?

When a business raises capital by issuing shares, the owners of those new shares are likely going to want to sell their stake someday. They may have a child going to college and need to cover the tuition bill. Perhaps they pass away, and their estate is subject to some hefty estate taxes. They may even leave it to their grandchildren (which brings about a form of generational wealth), but the heirs want to liquidate to buy a house. Whatever is driving their decision, they are not likely to tie up their funds unless they know somehow, someway, at some point in the future, that they will be able to find a buyer for their holdings without too much hassle. This is known as "the secondary market."

Without a stock exchange, these owners would have to go around to friends, family members, and community members, hoping to find someone to whom they could sell their shares. Technically, you can do this. You don't *have* to sell your shares on a stock exchange. You can take physical possession of your stocks in certificate form, endorse them, and sign them over to someone in exchange for payment. This can be done in a lawyer's office or at the dining room table if you are so inclined. The downside is that there is no transparency. Nobody knows what the best price is for a given stock at any given moment in time, in a market that operates like this. You could be selling your shares for $50 while someone in a next parish is getting $70. With a stock exchange, you will never know the person on the other end of the trade. The person could be halfway around the world. It could be a retired teacher. It could be a multi-billion-dollar insurance group. It could be me or it could be the newly financially savvy you.

THE JAMAICA CENTRAL SECURITIES DEPOSITORY (JCSD)

The Jamaica Central Securities Depository Limited (JCSD) is a wholly owned subsidiary of the Jamaica Stock Exchange (JSE) incorporated on January 8, 1998. The JCSD was established to provide depository and settlement services for securities traded electronically on the floor of the Jamaica Stock Exchange using a book entry system. This book entry system allows for easier and safer transfer of ownership since it eliminates the need to physically pass certificates from seller to buyer during a trade. The vision of the JCSD is that in 2020, the JCSD Group will be an efficient, independent and transparent employer of choice, service bureau for all brokers and central depository of knowledge for the securities market. Also commanding 90% Registry market share and 50 trustee clients; facilitating Six Hundred Billion Dollars ($600B) market capitalization and generating return on shareholders' equity of at least 10% above T-bill. The JCSD is divided into two Departments, the Depository Services Unit which has been operating since 1998 providing depository, custody and settlement services and the Registrar Services Unit which commenced its operations in March 2005 offering Registrar, Transfer and Capital Distribution Agent services.

The JCSD has one subsidiary, JCSD Trustee Services Limited which offers Trustee Services.

EQUITY

Simply put, equities are stock or shares of a company. When an investor buys a company's share, or equity, they gain ownership rights of that company. This entitles them to a certain percentage of any profits in the form of dividends, and to participate in the company's growth and expansion via voting rights at annual general meetings. However, the investors also bear the brunt of losses in case the company performs badly.

WHAT IS A STOCK?

A stock (also known as "shares" or "equity) is a type of security that signifies proportionate ownership in the issuing corporation. This entitles the stockholder to that proportion of the corporation's assets and earnings. It is buying ownership in a company which allows you an opportunity to receive dividend payment from profits made and a claim to assets in the case of liquidation.

Stocks are bought and sold predominantly on stock exchanges, though there can be private sales as well, and are the foundations of nearly every portfolio. These transactions must conform to government regulations which are meant to protect investors from fraudulent practices. The Jamaica Central Securities Depository Limited (JCSD) and the Regulatory & Market Oversight Division (RMOD) are responsible for enforcing safe practices and integrity in the stock market. Historically, stocks have outperformed most other investments over-the-long-run.

WHAT ARE SHARES?

Shares are units of ownership interest in a corporation or financial asset that provide for an equal distribution in any profits, if any are declared, in the form of dividends. The two main types of shares are common shares and preferred shares. In the past when shares were purchased in a company whether through an initial public offer or after the stock has been listed on the stock market for trading. Successful investors would get a paper detailing their share purchase and this paper was also a proof of ownership of shares. More recently, physical paper stock certificates have been replaced with electronic recording of stock shares. The shares purchased by an investor would be recorded on the Jamaica Central Securities Depository (JCSD) database.

DIFFERENCE BETWEEN A STOCK AND A SHARE

In today's markets, the distinction between stocks and shares has become blurred. Generally, the terms are interchangeable and refer to the piece of paper (no longer used) that denotes stock ownership, called a stock certificate. But there is a slight difference in the context to which each applies. The term "stock" describes the ownership certificates of any company (now electronic). While "shares" refers to the ownership certificates (electronic) of a specific company. If an investor says he or she owns stocks, that individual is referring to their overall ownership in a company, or multiple companies. If they say they own shares, the question then arises: shares in what company? The minor distinction between stocks and shares has more to do with syntax than financial or legal

accuracy. As a result, it's often ignored.

INITIAL PUBLIC OFFER (IPO)

One of the most vital things to know when it comes on to participating in an Initial Public Offering (IPO); is that you can send in your application for shares once the prospectus is out. This means that once the application form is available (it is found in the prospectus online or at a brokerage firm) you can go ahead and apply for shares long before the set date for the IPO to be opened. The application will be treated as an early application and will be processed on the IPO's opening date. That is, it will be treated as being received on the original opening date and time for the IPO. Just as going early is important, it is equally important not to wait until it is near the deadline date to subscribe. In doing so, you risk the stock being oversubscribed before the closing off date and as such making you unable to purchase any. In other words, "the early bird gets the most worms". Procrastination may also lead to not being able to subscribe for the desired amount. I would recommend going to your broker before the IPO date; if not, go within a week of the IPO being opened. I can speak from first-hand experience as I learnt about Wisynco's initial public offer late and when I got to the investment firm, my broker was only able to get 2000 shares and since then, the price per share has more than tripled at my time of writing.

Technology, like in most fields, is being used to make the way we conduct busy and our life in general, easier. One way this has come about is the launching of GoIpo by NCB Capital Markets. With this platform you can apply for an IPO online without having to go into the branch and without filling out any forms. It is a seamless process and even allows for early application. Also, there have been talks about NCB allowing the other brokerage firms access to the platform to process their IPO's.

WHAT TO DO IN THE CASE YOU MISSED AN INITIAL PUBLIC OFFER (IPO)

If the initial call of a company for the subscription of their shares was missed by either you finding out late, stock being oversubscribed (a lot more money being offered than what the company had proposed), not having the money at the time or by just plain right procrastination you can find solace in knowing that you are not alone. Many new investors and sometimes seasoned ones do miss the chance to purchase stocks at their IPO price. But not to worry if this ever happens to you because there is always the possibility of purchasing them after they have been listed on the Jamaican Stock Exchange. Buying shares after they have been listed has its advantages and disadvantages. Some stocks can almost double within a year or even a few months after listing. Others, on the other hand, will perform below their IPO price within that same time period of a year or even longer, depending on the demand for the stock.

PROSPECTUS

A prospectus is a formal legal document issued by a company when it is offering shares to the public. It normally contains the facts that an investor needs to make an informed investment decision such as a description of the company's business, financial statements, biographies of officers and directors, any litigation that is taking place, a list of material properties and any other material information. A prospectus issued in Jamaica must be approved by the Financial Services Commission and the Companies Offices of Jamaica and reviewed by the JSE to ensure that the information required for listing is contained in the prospectus. The JSE has up to 5 years of prospectuses on its website for general viewing.

MAKING MONEY FROM STOCKS

To be honest this is the real reason an investor would invest in a company. Money can be made in basically two ways. The first one is through dividend payments. Within the prospectus of a company's initial public offer lies an important bit of information that speaks to how often for the year dividends will be paid. The amount that will be paid is normally derived at a board of directors meeting. The second way to make money is through capital appreciation. Both will be further discussed in length.

CAPITAL APPRECIATION

Capital appreciation is a rise in the value of an asset based on a rise in market price. It occurs when the asset invested commands a higher price in the market than an investor originally paid for the asset. The capital appreciation portion of the investment includes all of the market value exceeding the original investment or cost basis. Capital appreciation is one of the two main sources of investment returns, with the others being dividend or interest income. The combination of capital appreciation with dividend or interest returns is referred to as total return. Capital appreciation can occur for many different reasons in different markets and asset classes. It can also occur with financial assets such as stocks or with real assets such as real estate.

DIVIDENDS

A dividend is the distribution of reward from a portion of a company's net profits and is paid to a class of its shareholders. Dividends are decided by the company's board of directors, though they must be approved by the shareholders through their voting rights. Dividends can be issued as cash payments via a cheque or an account deposit, and as shares of stock, though cash dividends are the most common. Along with companies, various mutual funds and Exchange-Traded Funds (ETF) also pay dividends. The frequency of dividend payment is determined by the company and can range from once per financial year to once per quarter (every three months).

RECEIVING DIVIDEND

PAYMENTS

When opening your account for the first time the broker will ask where you would like to receive your dividend payments. The choices given to you will generally include savings account, brokerage account or by cheque. At my first ever stock purchase (Wisynco's IPO), I had chosen that a cheque should be sent to the post office with my dividend earnings. But what I did not consider was that the payments would be small (depending on quantity of shares owned) and that going to the bank to change a cheque was not something I always liked doing. It turned out however that I never went to the post office and the cheques were sent back to the JCSD. When I called the JCSD, I was instructed to send an email to where I would want the uncollected and future dividend payments for all the stocks of all the companies in my portfolio to be sent. This time I smartly chose that the payments be disbursed in my savings account at JMMB. Choosing a savings or a brokerage account will allow you to be able to readily reinvest the earnings into buying more stocks. One downside in not making this decision earlier was that the Jamaica Central Security Depository has not rectified all the issues I have had with dividends owed to me and it has been two months.

BROKERAGE ACCOUNT

A stockbroker (broker) is a direct link between the client and the stock market. Orders to buy and sell securities on the stock exchange are handled exclusively by this person. Brokers buy or sell shares on behalf of their clients. Brokers participate electronically on the Trading (Platform) Floor and have advanced tools (the technology) to assist them in handling trades on behalf of their clients. The stockbroker operates from a firm that is normally called a brokerage house and is registered by the Jamaica Stock Exchange and approved by the Financial Services Commission (FSC), hence the name Broker Member or Member Dealer. Currently there are twelve Broker Members or Member Dealers that are registered by the JSE to conduct business on behalf of their clients.

JSE Brokers

- Barita Investments Limited

- Credit Union Fund Management Company (CUFM)

- GK Capital Management Limited

- JMMB Securities Limited

- JN Fund Managers Limited

- M/VL Stockbrokers Limited

- Mayberry Investments Limited

- NCB Capital Markets Limited

- Proven Wealth Limited

- Sagicor Investments Jamaica Limited

- Scotia Investments Jamaica Limited

- Stocks and Securities Limited (SSL)

- Victoria Mutual Wealth Management Limited

ORDER

An order is an investor's instructions to a broker or brokerage firm to purchase or sell a security on the investor's behalf. Orders are typically placed over the phone or online through a trading platform, but can also be placed in person. Orders fall into different available types which allow you to place restrictions on your orders affecting the price and time at which the order can be executed. These order instructions will affect your profit or loss on the transaction, and in some cases, whether the order is executed at all.

The exchange trade securities through a bid/ask process. This means that to sell, there must be a buyer willing to pay the selling price. While also to buy, there must be a seller willing to sell at the buying price. Unless a buyer and a seller come together at the same price, no transaction occurs.

The bid is the highest advertised price someone is will to pay for an asset, while the ask price is the lowest advertised price someone is willing to sell an asset at. The bid and ask are constantly changing, as each bid and offer represents an order. As orders are filled, the levels will change. For example, if there is a bid at 25.25 and another at 25.26, when all the orders at 25.26 have been filled, the next highest bid is 25.25.

This bid/ask process is important to keep in mind when placing an order, as the type of order selected will impact the price the trade is filled at, when it will be filled, or whether it will be filled at all. I know that JMMB on their online trading platform allows you to select different order types.

On most markets, orders are accepted from both individual and institutional investors, and the same applies to the Jamaican market. Most individuals trade through broker-dealers which require them to place one of many order types when making a trade. But you can also trade through the stock exchanges online platform called the J-Trader Pro which allows you to get around commission fees. The drawback to this is that not all brokers are listed on this platform and only listed ones can allow their clients to use the platform.

The brokers listed include:

- Barita Investments Ltd.

- GK Capital Management Ltd.

- M/VL Stockbrokers Ltd.

- NCB Capital Markets Ltd.

- Sagicor Investments

- VM Wealth Management

NCB to date is very hard to deal with when it comes on to them accepting your account on the platform and in responding to your funds-in requests. It has been a week since I have made both requests and none has been

accepted for me to start trading on the J-Trader platform.

WHEN A TRADE IS MADE

In financial markets, trading refers to the buying and selling of securities, such as the purchase of stock on the floor of the Jamaica Stock Exchange (JSE).

Initially, it used to take investors four business days before their newly purchased stocks could be reflected in their equity account (T+3). Now it will only take three days. This shortened time is called T+2 and refers to the trade date (the 'T') plus 2 business days (+2) to complete the transaction and for it to reflect in your equity portfolio.

When investing on the Jamaican Stock Market there are a lot of different brokerage firms out there that provide different levels of freedom and autonomy depending on which one you choose.

THE FOCUS SHOULD BE ON YOU!

The firm you choose should not be just because your friend uses it or that you already have a savings or chequings account with them. When it comes on to you and investing; you should be entirely selfish and care 100% about you. The only time you should care about the firm of your choice is if they are listed on the stock market and you have bought ownership into their company. Even then you are still putting yourself first because their actions or handlings of the company will directly affect stock prices. A bank's sole purpose like many other businesses is to make a profit, whether we know how they do it or not, and their subsidiary (investment arm in this case) is no different.

YOUR CHOICE OF FIRM

The broker of choice is dependent on a couple of factors that includes: your income/savings, risk tolerance, knowledge of the stock market, what your long-term goals are and how much control you want over your portfolio; among other things. For example, a person earning a salary of JMD $60,000-$70,000, you should not start at Mayberry Investments as their minimum requirement is half a million dollars. But even if you make less than that you should not be deterred. One way of looking at it is that a lot of us as Jamaicans throw partner that is worth $10,000 per hand per month whether we have a stable income. So, if you look at it in this light it is quite clear that it is possible to put money aside to invest in stocks for your future benefit. With that said though, you can open your brokerage account with as little as $5,000 or smaller depending on whether you are opening during an IPO.

What this means is that if the minimum buy in for an IPO is less than $5,000 you can open your account with just the minimum amount for the IPO. Brokers such as the National Commercial Bank Capital Markets (NCBCM), Sagicor Investments and Jamaica Money Market Brokers (JMMB) Group provide equity accounts for persons who are unable to get to such high minimum requirements of a half a million or greater.

THE INVESTOR THAT DOES

NOT HAVE THE TIME

Not to worry there is a way for you to partake in the growing economy and the number one performing stock exchange in the world for 2015 and 2018 just the same. Yup, you read the right thing. No typographical error and your mind did not just play a trick on you. It is true that our little island in the Caribbean, Jamaica, possesses the best performing stock exchange in the world and is forecasted to get better with an improving economy. The way in which you can take full advantage of the stock market even though you might have a busy schedule with little to no time to check on your stocks is by having a managed portfolio. This means that a portfolio manager will study the market and provide recommendations, which will allow you to make decisions on stock purchases. Simply put you have a professional that uses his knowledge and expertise in the stock market to make your money work for you. As you may have already figured out this will come at a higher cost than if you did it yourself, but the returns will pay off in medium to long term.

YOU ARE NOW AN

INVESTOR!!!

After doing all the necessary research and following the teachings of this book, I strongly believe that you are fully equipped to open your equity account and start investing. While you are now a "young" investor and have started to purchase ownership in the companies of interest to you; you are never truly an investor unless you continue to develop yourself, (if you get what I am saying). One way I would recommend in doing this is to read the books that I have read and have mentioned above. Currently, I am reading 'The Intelligent Investor" by Benjamin Graham; a book that even the great Warren Buffet hails as "the best book on investing". If you don't know who Warren Buffet is; simply put, he is an investment guru and someone I recommend you should follow.

TIPS FROM ONE "YOUNG INVESTOR" TO ANOTHER

1. Use your Social Media accounts as your plug into a myriad of investment knowledge.

2. Download apps such as InvestEd to educate yourself more and improve your knowledge on investing in general.

3. Follow all the companies you have ownership in. An easy way to do this is to find them on Instagram, Twitter and Facebook to keep track on major deals or happenings. Whatever acquisitions, sales or partnerships the company is successful in will be communicated via social media and will affect its stock price.

4. Download the Jamaica Stock Exchange (JSE) app to keep track of the daily closing market prices, get live market price changes during trading hours and the latest news on what is happening with the listed companies. You can also view the JSE's website to gain access to newly released prospectuses for upcoming IPO's.

5. Follow as much financial institutions as possible to keep abreast of any new initial public offerings that might be of interest to you. The same applies to following the JSE.

6. Set aside 10% of your earnings or salary for investment and/or another 10% for savings. In either case this is called paying yourself first.

7. Never ask your broker to buy at market price! The price that he or she pays for it just might upset you. What I would recommend is that you ask the broker to buy at a limit price that you would have communicated.

8. Read! This tip cannot be emphasised enough. The more you learn about investment and its strategies, the more likely you are to reap massive gains.

9. "Buy when others are selling". I stumbled upon this tip and find the strategy to be very slick. I do advise however, that you are never to just simply buy because the stock price is falling. Only apply this if you are confident that the falling stock price of the company that you are buying into will eventually rebound.

10. Never take a loan from a financial institution to buy stocks. Even though persons have done this and have successfully benefitted, I do not recommend this type of approach for a young investor especially one with little to no savings or experience. Say the stock does rise then it will take at least a year or even longer. You would have to be able to afford to make payments on principal amount borrowed along with interest, while you wait for the stock to reach a profitable price.

11. Use other people's money to make money. This tip is very dear to me as I stumbled upon it at a time in which I needed more money than I currently had to subscribe for shares in upcoming IPO's. With this rule it allowed me to stay true to tip number 10 of not borrowing money (from the bank) to make

money. Instead, try fundraising the money, and if you do borrow try to source from friends that will allow you to get very good if any at all interest rates.

12. This next tip you may have heard at school or functions or even through an informal reasoning with a friend; but the value of it should never be underestimated. This tip will ultimately determine how far you will reach and to a larger extent your tenure in investing. It speaks to your support system along with having a "sample" of your mastermind group. Are you ready for it? Alright here goes. Surround yourself with persons that are likeminded and are trotting on the same path as you are. This tip like many given in this book is not directed to only investing but can be applied to all facets of your life for improved success.

13. The Jamaica Stocks Watch App is a great app to track the Stock Exchange.

14. The JSE has a wealth of knowledge and resources so take part in them and develop yourself.

15. PDF version of the Jamaica Stock Exchange little blue book. file:///E:/Investment%20in%20Jamaica/A-Guide-to-Jamaica-Securities-Markets.pdf

16. Good information and patience are the key in the stock market.

17. Lastly, I am going to leave a website with you. This is basically a blog where investors come together and share their findings and research (like a wikipedia). Here it is IC INSIDER http://icinsider.com/.

REFERENCE LIST

1. https://economictimes.indiatimes.com/markets/stocks/news/are-equity-and-stock-the-same/articleshow/59530817.cms

2. https://www.quora.com/What-does-equity-mean-in-the-stock-market

3. https://www.investopedia.com/terms/s/stock.asp

4. https://www.investopedia.com/terms/s/shares.asp

5. https://www.investopedia.com/video/play/whats-difference-between-shares-and-stocks/

6. https://www.investopedia.com/terms/d/dividend.asp

7. https://www.thebalance.com/what-is-a-stock-exchange-358113

8. https://www.jamstockex.com/about/jse-subsidiaries/jamaica-central-securities-depository/

9. https://www.investopedia.com/terms/c/capitalappreciation.asp

10. https://www.investopedia.com/terms/o/order.asp

11. https://www.jamstockex.com/investor-centre/

12. https://www.jamstockex.com/investor-centre/jse-brokers/

www.ingramcontent.com/pod-product-compliance
Lightning Source LLC
Chambersburg PA
CBHW021930170526
45157CB00005B/2260